SPHYNX

MARYSA STORM

Black Rabbit Books

Bolt Jr. is published by Black Rabbit Books
P.O. Box 227, Mankato, Minnesota, 56002.
www.blackrabbitbooks.com
Copyright © 2025 Black Rabbit Books

Alissa Thielges, editor
Rhea Magaro, designer

All rights reserved. No part of this book may be reproduced in any form without written permission from the publisher.

Names: Storm, Marysa, author.
Title: Sphynx / by Marysa Storm.
Description: Mankato, MN : Black Rabbit Books, [2025] | Series: Bolt Jr. Our favorite cats | Includes bibliographical references and index. | Audience: Ages 5–8 | Audience: Grades K–1
Identifiers: LCCN 2024010397 (print) | LCCN 2024010398 (ebook) | ISBN 9781644666814 (library binding) | ISBN 9781644666999 (ebook)
Subjects: LCSH: Sphynx cat—Juvenile literature.
Classification: LCC SF449.S68 S76 2025 (print) | LCC SF449.S68 (ebook) | DDC 636.8--dc23/eng/20240408
LC record available at https://lccn.loc.gov/2024010397
LC ebook record available at https://lccn.loc.gov/202401039

Image Credits

Dreamstime/David Tadevosian, 20–21; Shutterstock/Alexander Piragis, 1, 6, Eric Isselee, 4, 20, Gladkova Svetlana, 13, Jesus Vivas Alacid, 5, kapichka, 11, Katrin Baidimirova, cover, Kekyalyaynen, 23, Kirill Vorobyev, 10, Liza_Bird, 19, Nynke van Holten, 7, Polina Tomtosova, 3, 24, serhii.suravikin, 17, siridhata, 15, slowmotiongli, 12, Studio-N, 8–9, Sviatoslav_Shevchenko, 18

Contents

Chapter 1
Meet the Sphynx......4

Chapter 2
Personality...........10

Chapter 3
Sphynx Care.........16

More Information.........22

CHAPTER 1

Meet the Sphynx

It's a cold day. A boy curls up in a big blanket. He is nice and **toasty**. His sphynx cat comes over. It is a hairless cat. It pushes its way into the blanket. Time to snuggle!

toasty: comfortably warm

Sphynx ◀ .... COMPARING WEIGHTS
6 to 12 pounds

Special Cats

These sweet cats look a little different than others. A short fuzz covers their bodies. But they look hairless. Their skin is wrinkly. Their eyes and ears are big. Their tails are thin like rope.

▶ **Ragdoll**
10 to 20 pounds
(4.5 to 9 kg)

PARTS OF A Sphynx

large ears

big eyes

paws

8

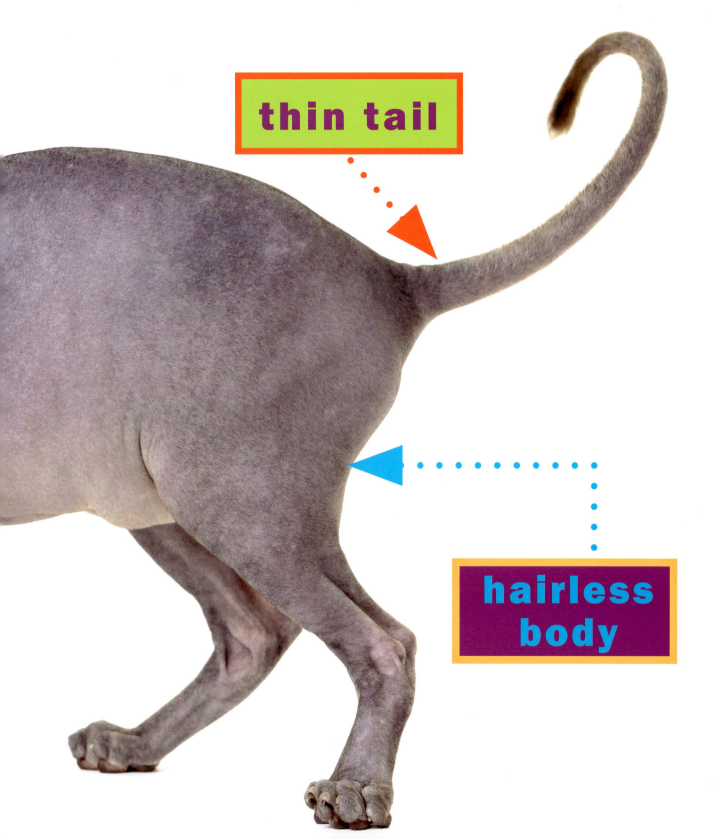

CHAPTER 2

Sphynx cats are **loyal**. They love to be around their owners. It doesn't matter if they are playing or cuddling. But don't leave them alone for long. They can get into trouble. They might scratch things they shouldn't.

loyal: constant support for someone or something

FACT These cats get along with other cats and nice dogs.

Curious Cats

These cats are curious. If something catches their attention, they will **investigate**. Sphynx cats are also active. They have a lot of energy. They love to climb. They have strong legs.

investigate: to find out information about something

Where They Came From

Sphynx cats are from Canada.

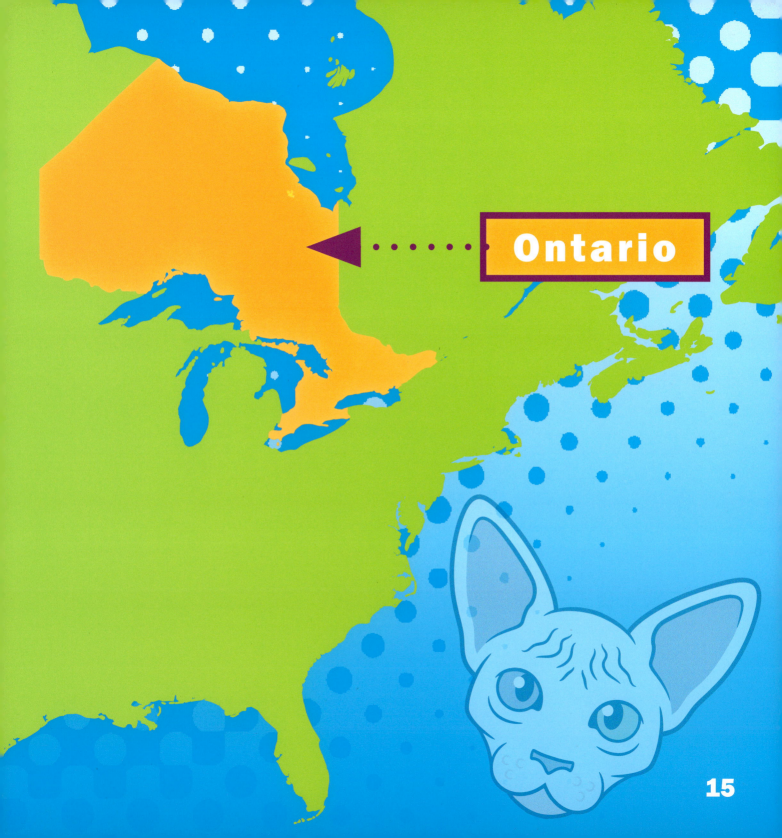

CHAPTER 3

Sphynx Care

Sphynx cats need food and water. They also need special care. Oil builds up on their skin. Owners must wash their cats weekly. This washing removes the oil.

The cats need their teeth brushed too.

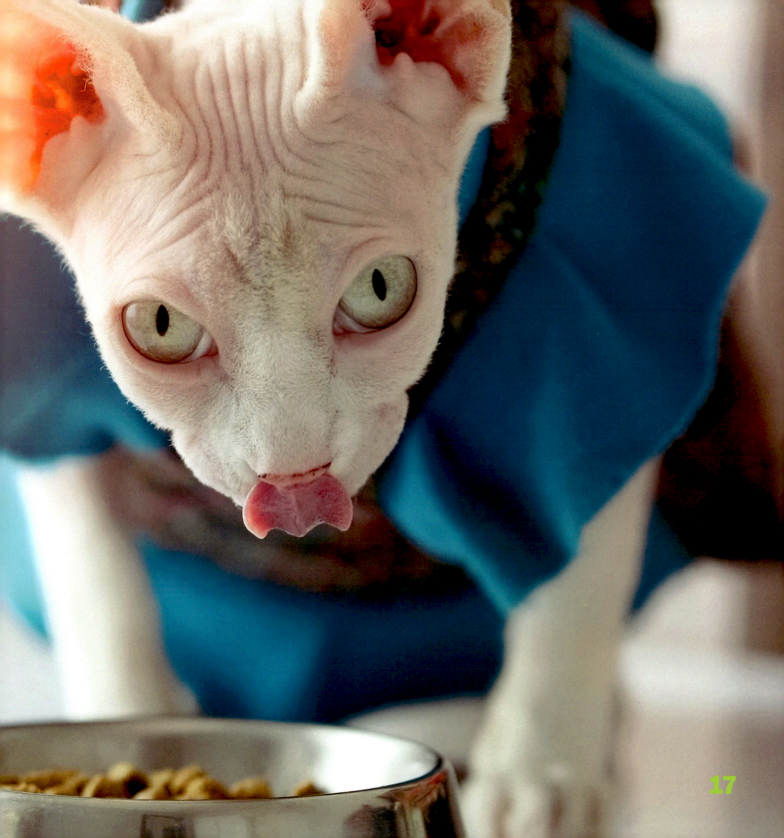

Friends for Life

Sphynx cats need extra care. But owners say they are worth it. They love these sweet, playful cats. The cats love to be held and petted. They make great cuddle buddies.

Sphynx's Height
8 to 10 inches
(20–25 centimeters) tall

Bonus Facts

It is easy for these cats to get **sunburned**.

sunburn: red and sore skin from too much sunlight

The first hairless cat was born in 1966.

READ MORE/WEBSITES

Burling, Alexis. *Cats.* Minneapolis: Abdo Publishing Company, 2024.

MacMillan, Kathy. *Cats.* Minneapolis: Early Encyclopedias, 2023.

Wilson, Sierra. *Sphynx.* New York: Lightbox Learning Inc., 2023.

Sphynx
https://kids.britannica.com/students/article/sphynx/313596

Sphynx Cat Facts for Kids
https://kids.kiddle.co/Sphynx_cat

Sphynx Cat Facts & Worksheets
https://kidskonnect.com/animals/sphynx-cat

GLOSSARY

investigate (in-VES-tuh-gayt)—to find out information about something

loyal (LOY-uhl)—having constant support for someone or something

sunburn (SUHN-burn)—red and sore skin from too much sunlight

toasty (TOH-stee)—comfortably warm

INDEX

B
body parts, 7, 8–9

C
care, 16, 19
climbing, 13
coat, 4, 7, 9

L
life span, 21

O
origin, 14–15, 20, 21

P
personality, 4, 10, 11, 13, 19

S
size, 6–7, 19